HAL•LEONARD

HARMONICA PLAY-ALONG

VOL. 14

JAZZ STANDARDS

for C Chromatic Harmonica

ISBN 978-1-4234-7553-8

Visit Hal Leonard Online at
www.halleonard.com

HAL•LEONARD®
CORPORATION
7777 W. BLUEMOUND RD. P.O. BOX 13819
MILWAUKEE, WISCONSIN 53213

Dear fellow harmonica players,

Playing jazz on the chromatic harmonica is one of the great pleasures of my life, and with this volume, I hope I can help you develop your skills and your enjoyment of this endlessly engaging pursuit.

In this volume you will find two versions of each song. The first is of me playing along with the Hal Leonard rhythm section tracks; the second is just the rhythm tracks without me, for you to play over.

In my performances, I have attempted to demonstrate some of the principles of jazz interpretation and improvisation that are important to me. Some of these are:

Tone
Because playing jazz on the harmonica is such a challenge in itself, some players overlook the importance of the overall tone they produce. Good harmonica tone is produced by proper embouchure (mouth position) and breathing technique. Using an appropriate microphone–with EQ and effect for amplifying and/or recording–is important, but it will not make up for weak acoustic tone.

Interpretation of Melody
One good way for beginners to approach improvisation is simply to interpret the melody in a personal way. The melodies on this CD are all played with my personal interpretation, but I encourage you to play the melodies as you feel them. While it's important to play the correct notes of the original melody, your phrasing and ornamentation of those notes is largely what defines your unique style as a jazz musician.

For beginning improvisers, embellishment of the melody can be a first step, which does not require a deep knowledge of jazz harmony. Just follow your ear, and your emotions.

Motif-Based Improvisation
Many of the improvisations on this CD are "motif-based," meaning that a small musical idea (motif) presented early in the solo is developed throughout the chorus. Most great composed melodies are motif-based, because motifs give a melody coherence. For example, the melody of "Autumn Leaves" begins with the motif G, A, Bb, Eb, which is then repeated three times, altered each time to fit the underlying harmony.

Since improvisation is the art of creating spontaneous melodies over chord changes, a good improvised melody also needs motifs to be coherent. In my first improvised chorus of "Autumn Leaves" for example, the opening motif is like the melody's first phrase, but with a twist: the final note goes down instead of up. Then the motif gets stretched, inverted, and mangled in various other ways.

Playing Technique and Phrasing
While teaching harmonica technique is outside the scope of the book, the harmonica tablature can give a good idea of how I executed the more challenging passages in my improvisations. Because there are alternate ways of playing Fs and Cs on the chromatic, many phrases can be played in several different ways. I took care to play my improvisations in the most efficient and musical way I could, and these choices are reflected in the tablature. If a phrase seems very difficult to play, try following the tablature; it may become easier.

Learning which F and which C to play in a particular passage is an important part of harmonica technique. The "blow and draw" action of the harmonica makes playing smooth legato lines a real challenge. Finding the most efficient way to play the alternate Fs and Cs can help avoid a "choppy" phrasing.

Finally, while you are very welcome to learn and perform my entire solos if they appeal to you, the real point of this book/CD package is to help you evolve your own "voice" on the instrument. I hope that my solos will show you some ideas that I came up with, and inspire you to discover your own. Although it may seem constrained by its unusual design and playing technique, the harmonica is capable of far more musical nuance and virtuosity than we can imagine.

—Will Galison

JAZZ STANDARDS

CONTENTS

Autumn Leaves

English lyric by Johnny Mercer
French lyric by Jacques Prevert
Music by Joseph Kosma

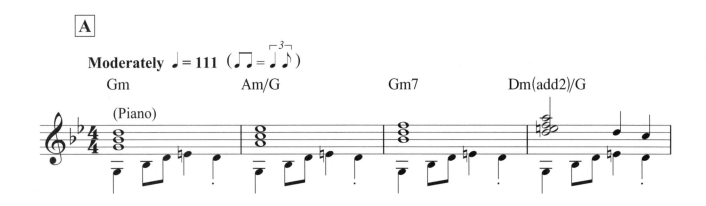

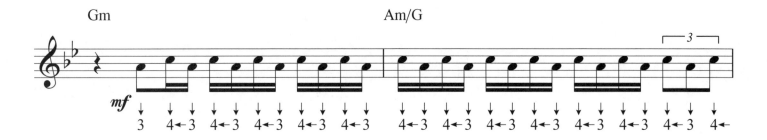

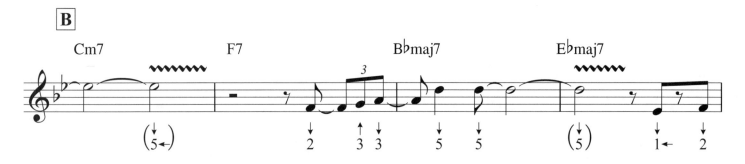

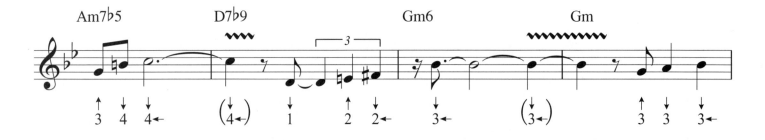

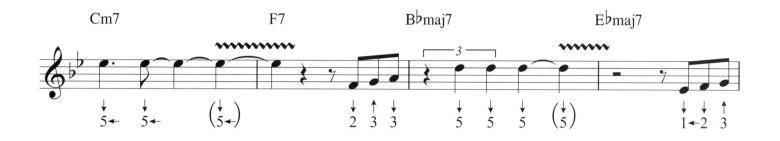

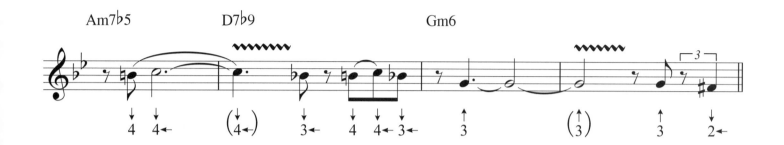

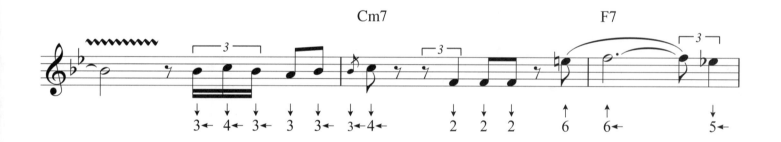

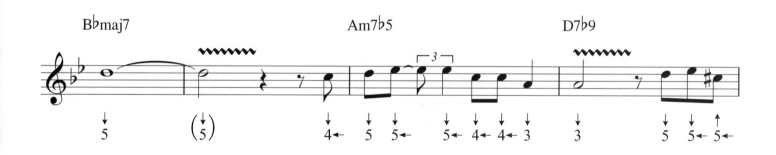

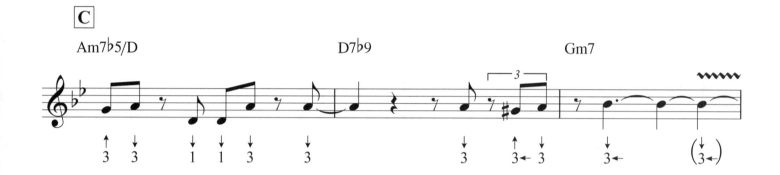

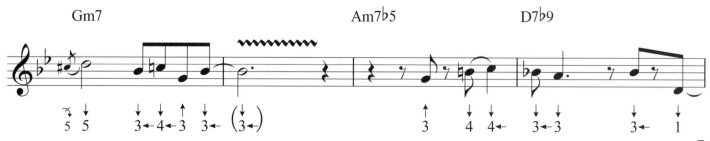

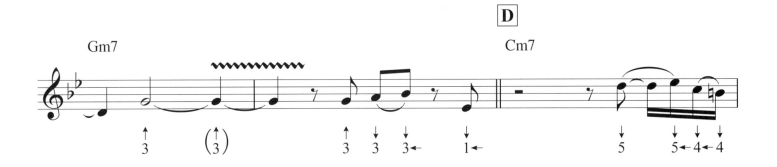

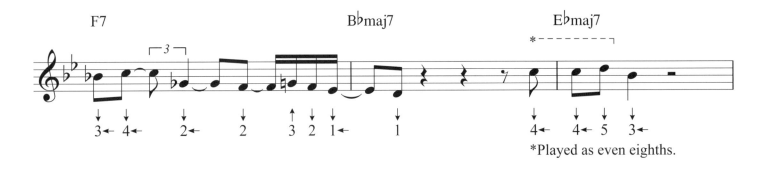

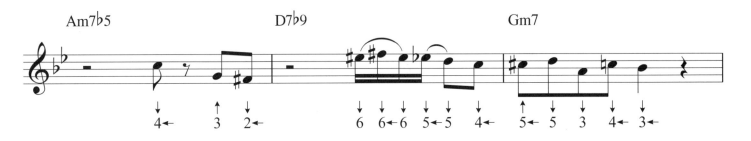

*Played as even eighths.

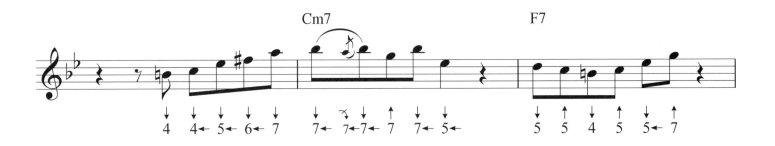

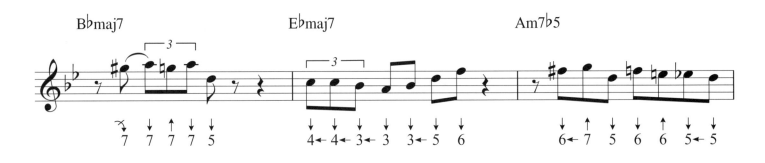

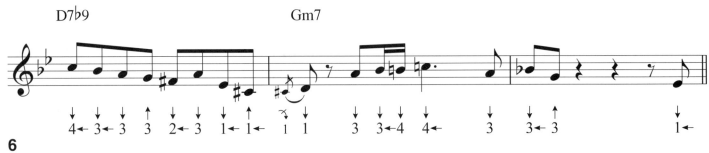

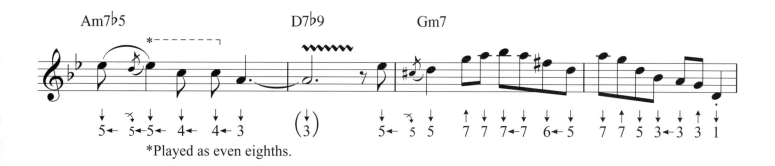

*Played as even eighths.

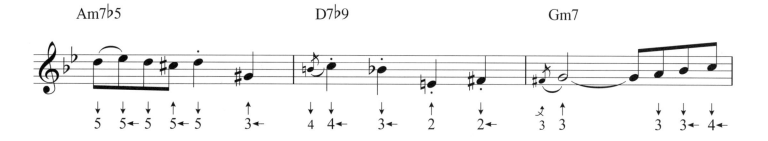

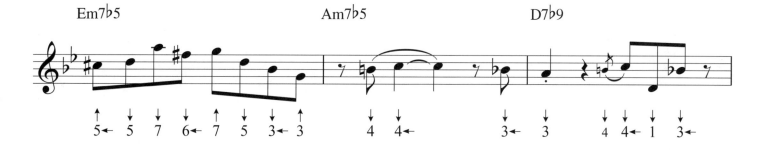

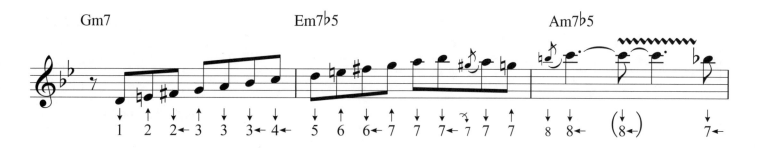

Free time

Georgia on My Mind

Words by Stuart Gorrell
Music by Hoagy Carmichael

*Played behind the beat.

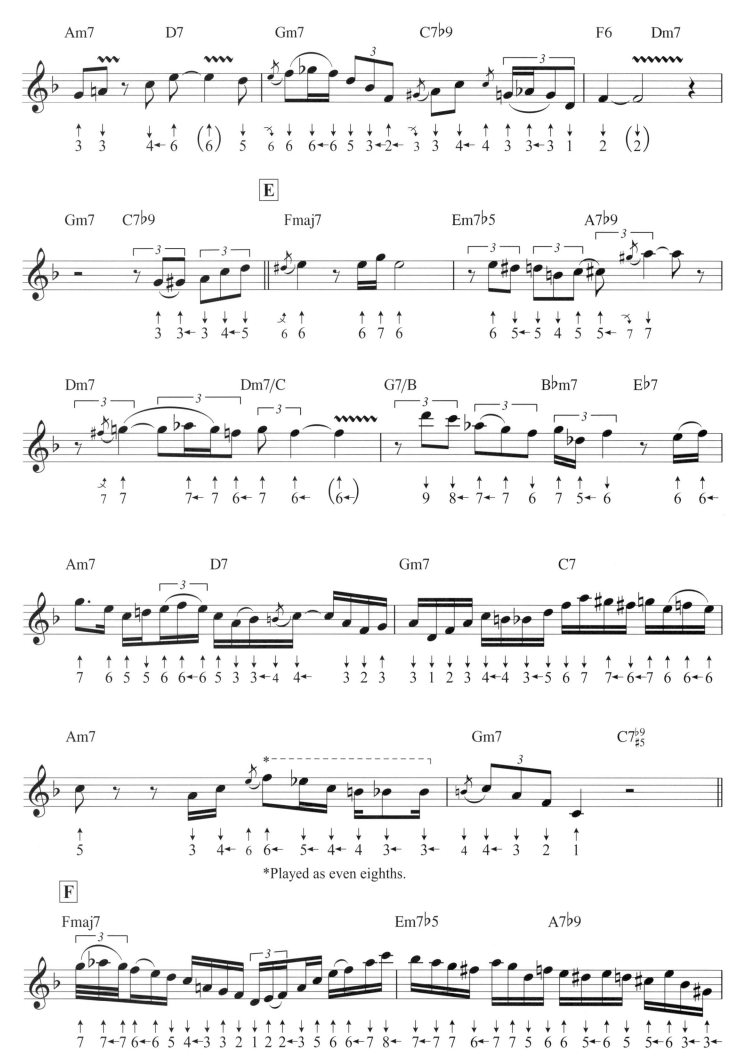

*Played as even eighths.

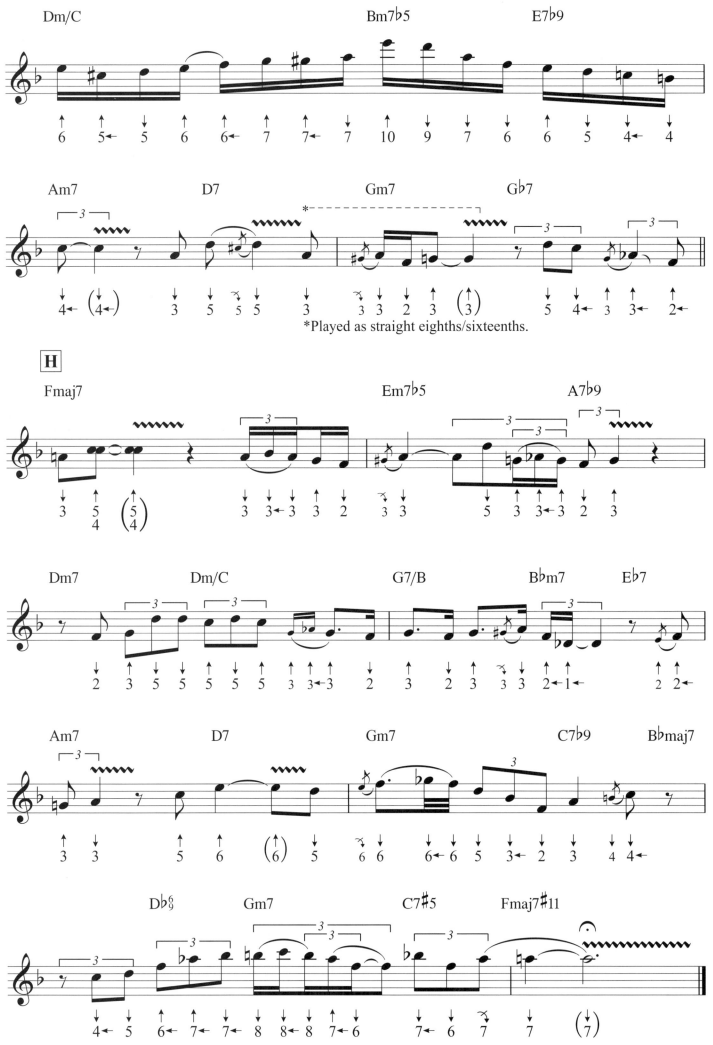

*Played as straight eighths/sixteenths.

Lullaby of Birdland

Words by George David Weiss
Music by George Shearing

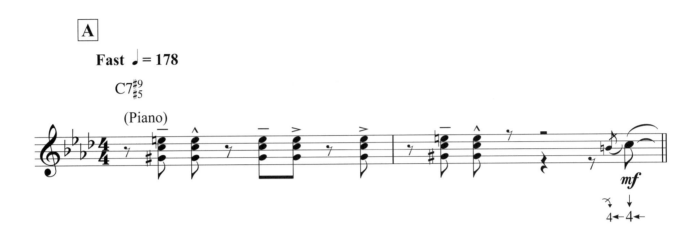

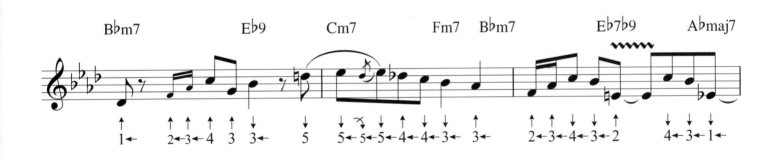

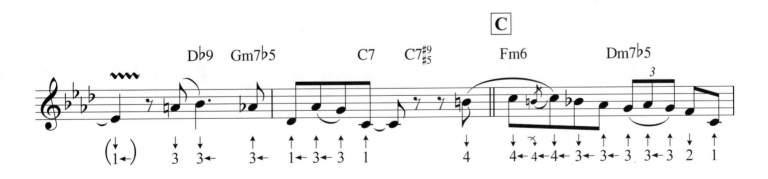

16

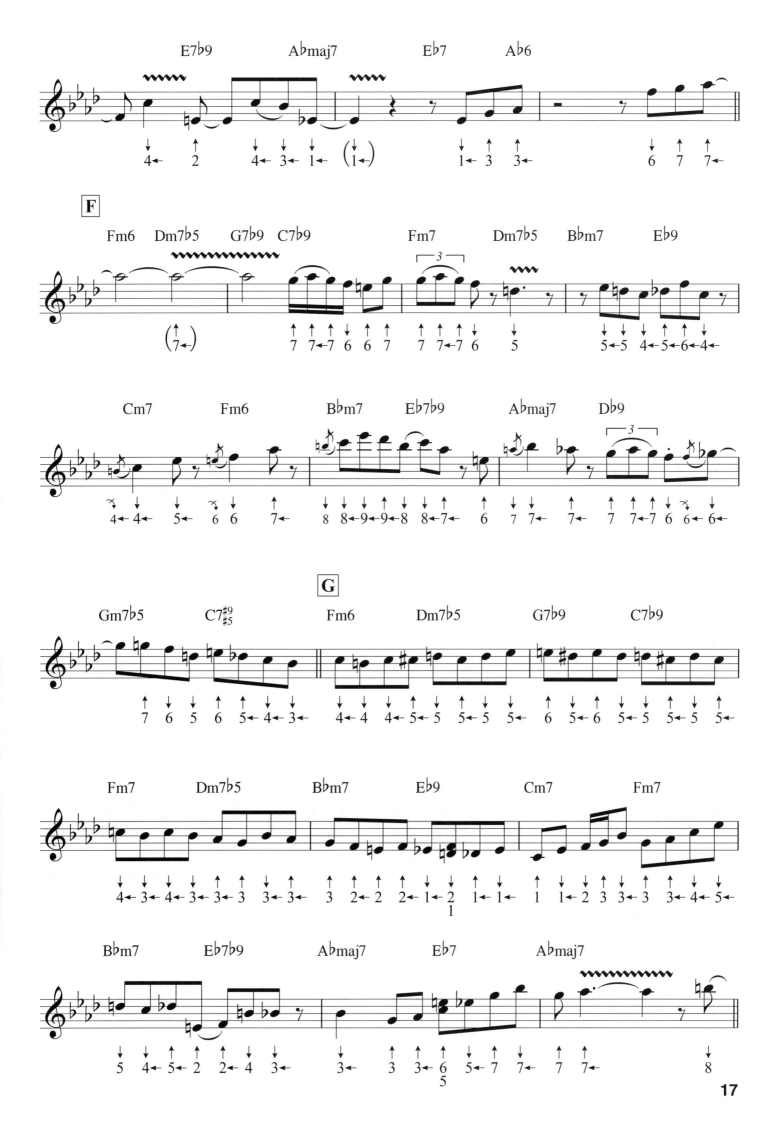

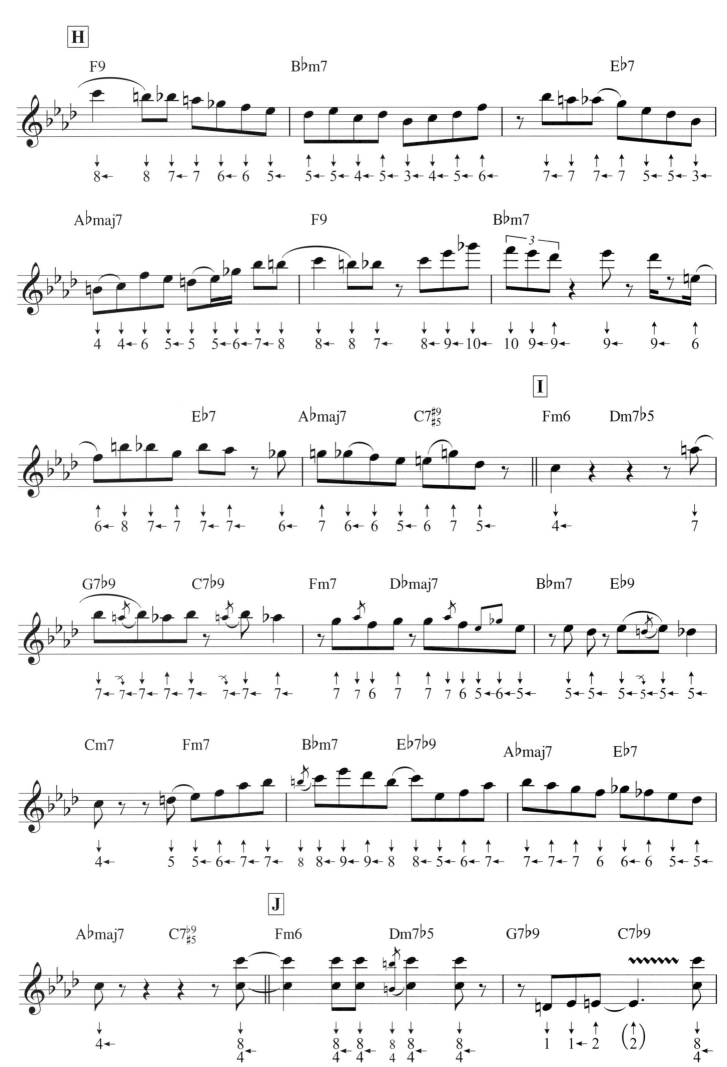

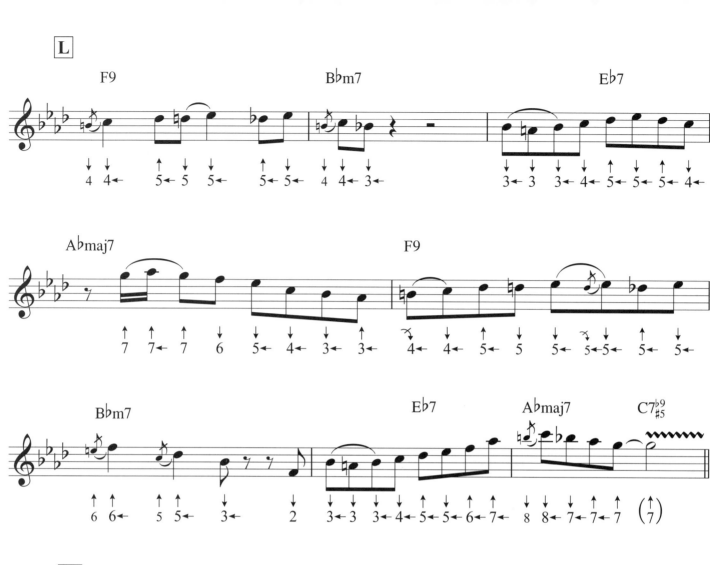

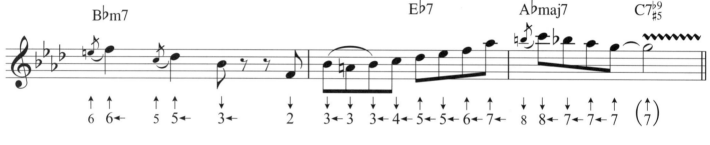

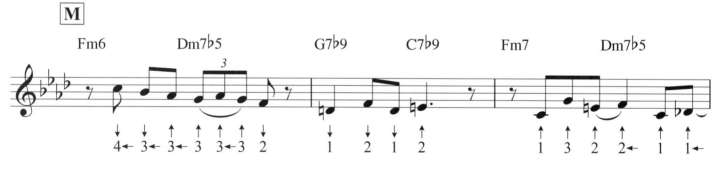

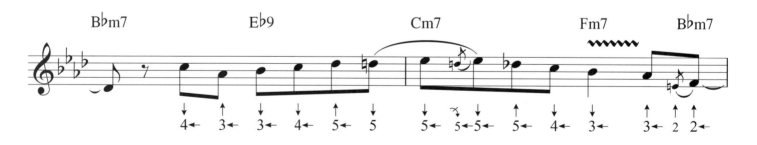

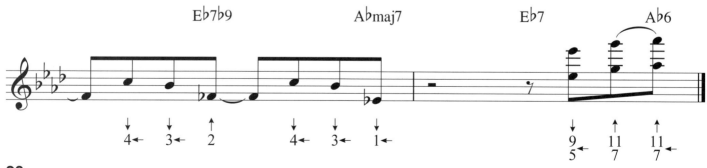

Meditation
(Meditação)

Music by Antonio Carlos Jobim
Original Words by Newton Mendonça
English Words by Norman Gimbel

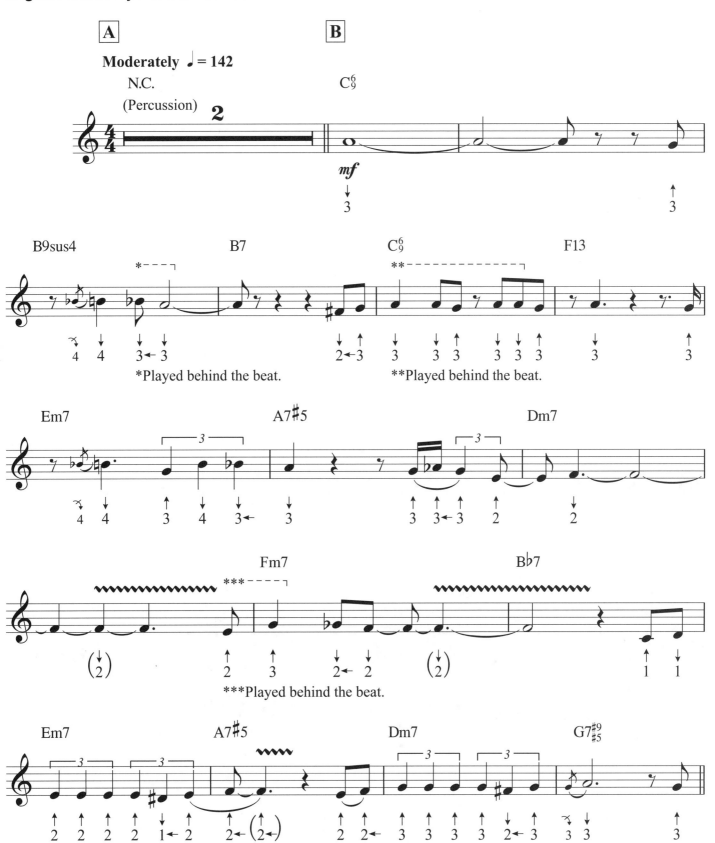

*Played behind the beat.

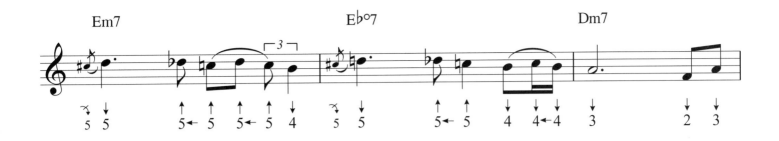

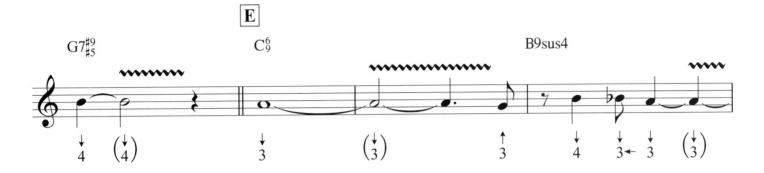

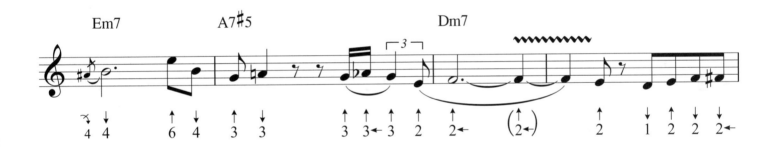

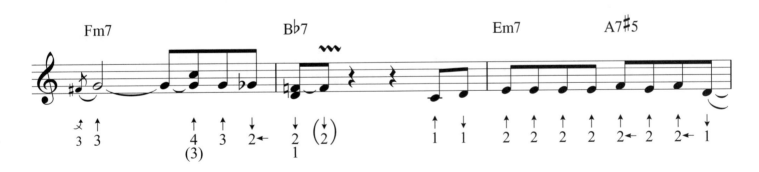

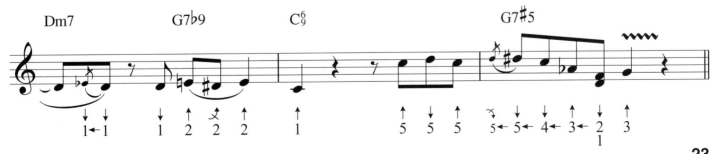

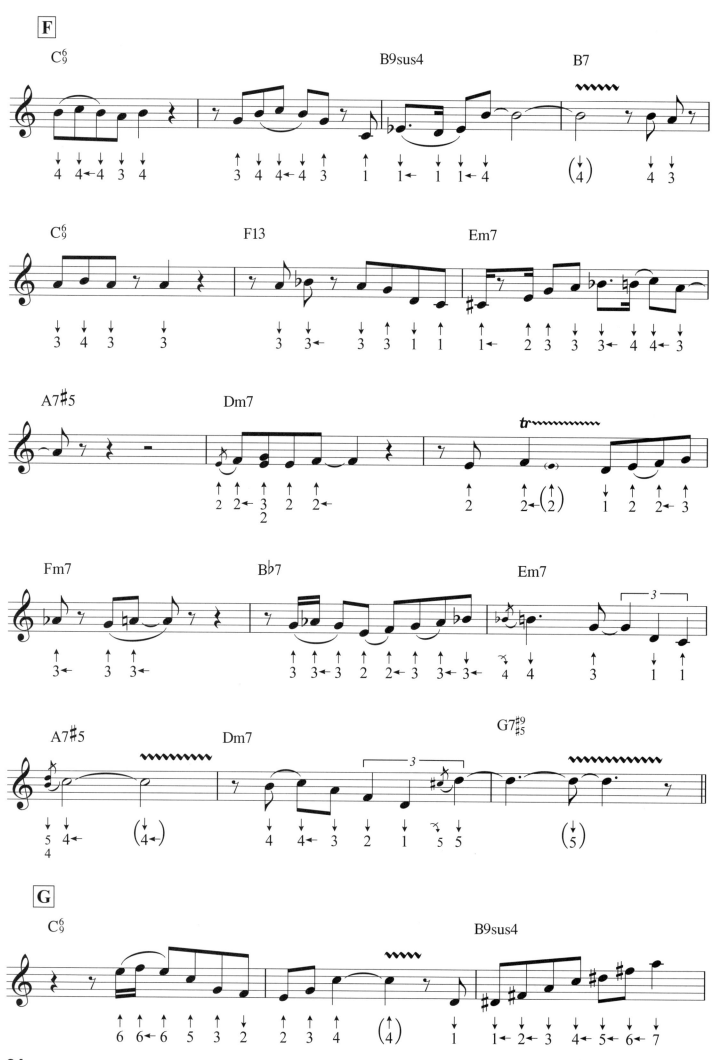

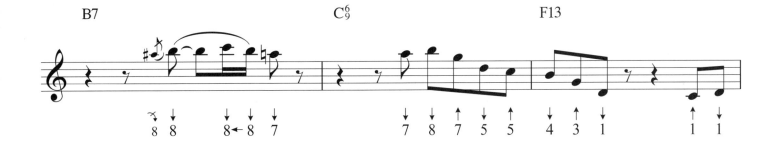

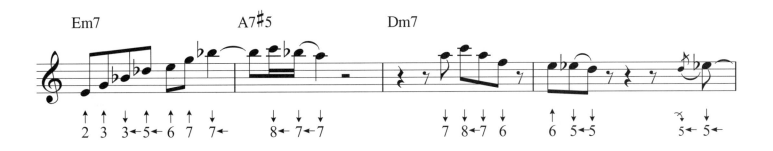

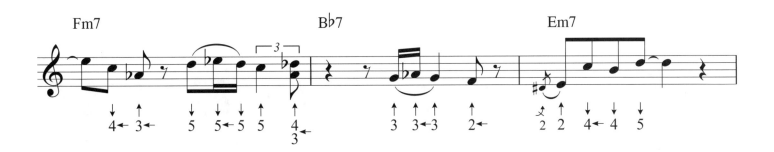

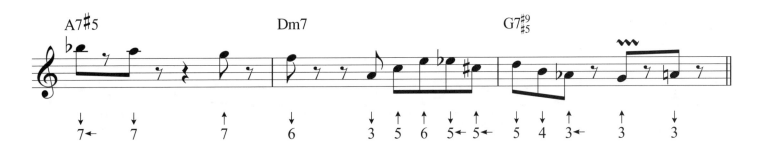

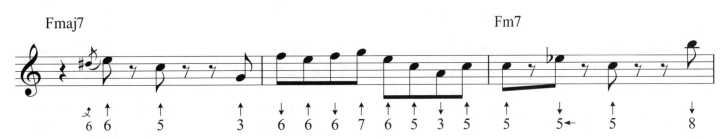

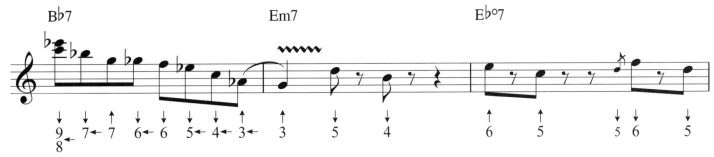

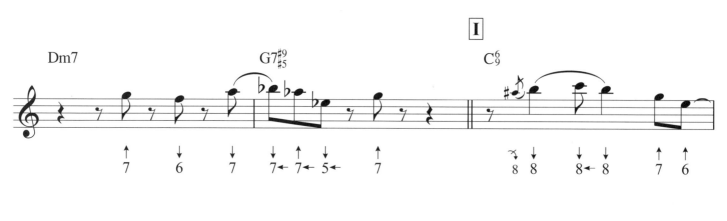

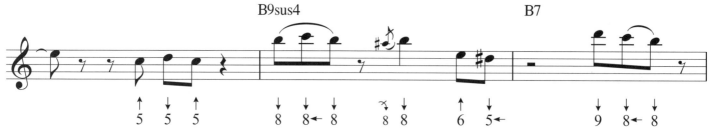

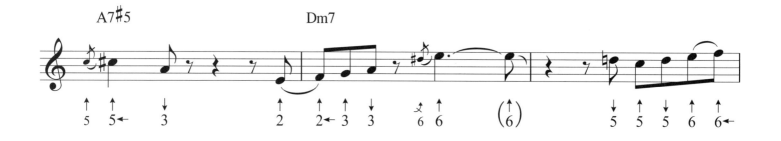

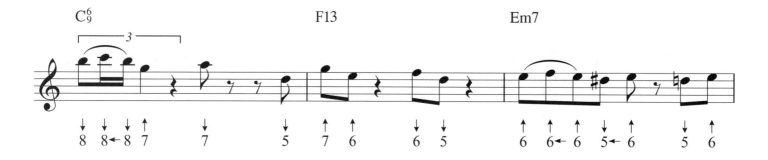

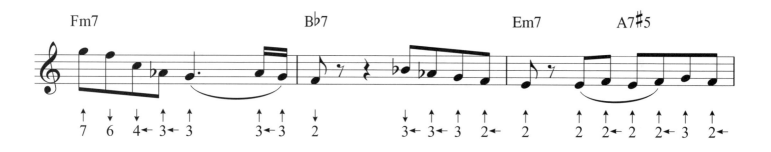

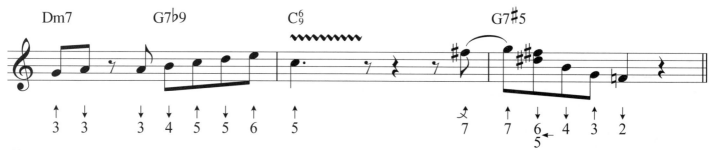

*Played
behind
the beat.

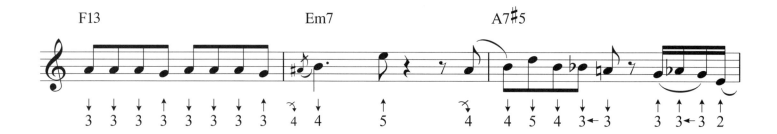

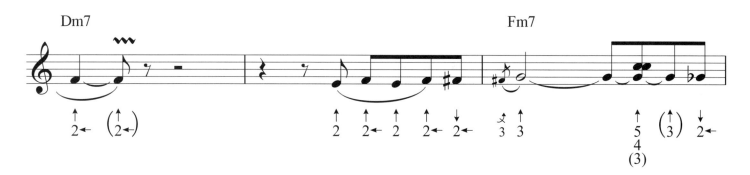

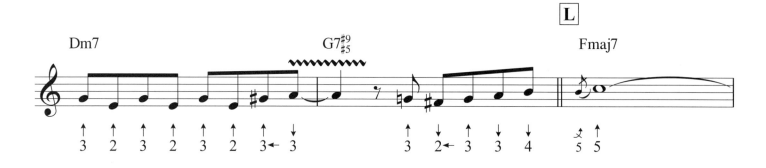

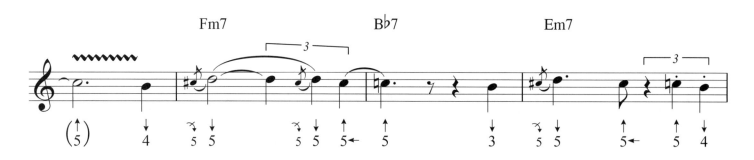

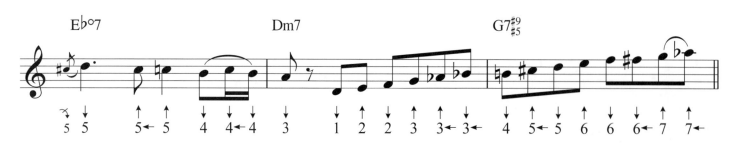

My Funny Valentine

Words by Lorenz Hart
Music by Richard Rodgers

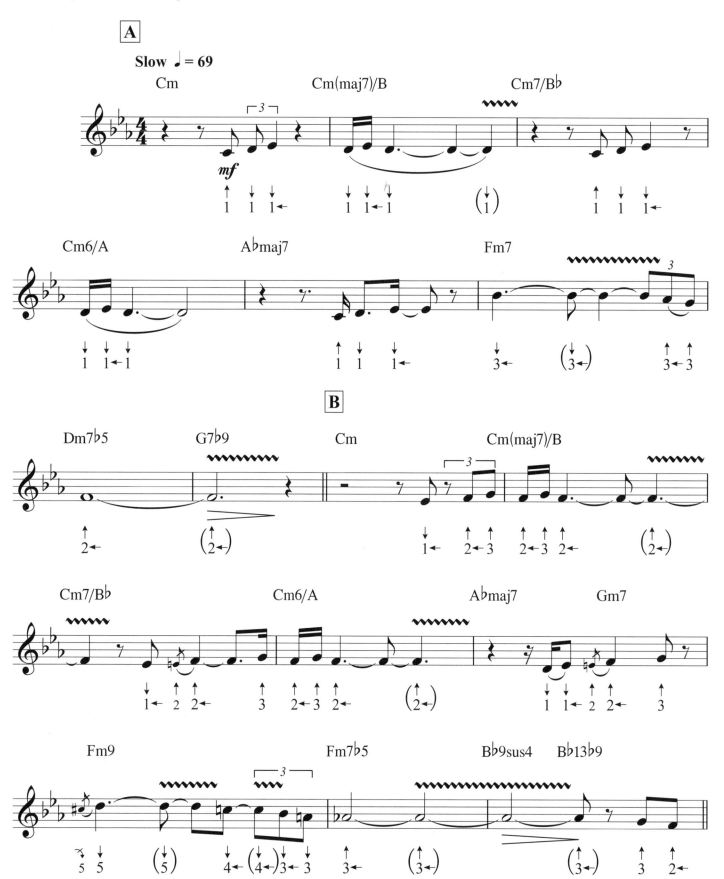

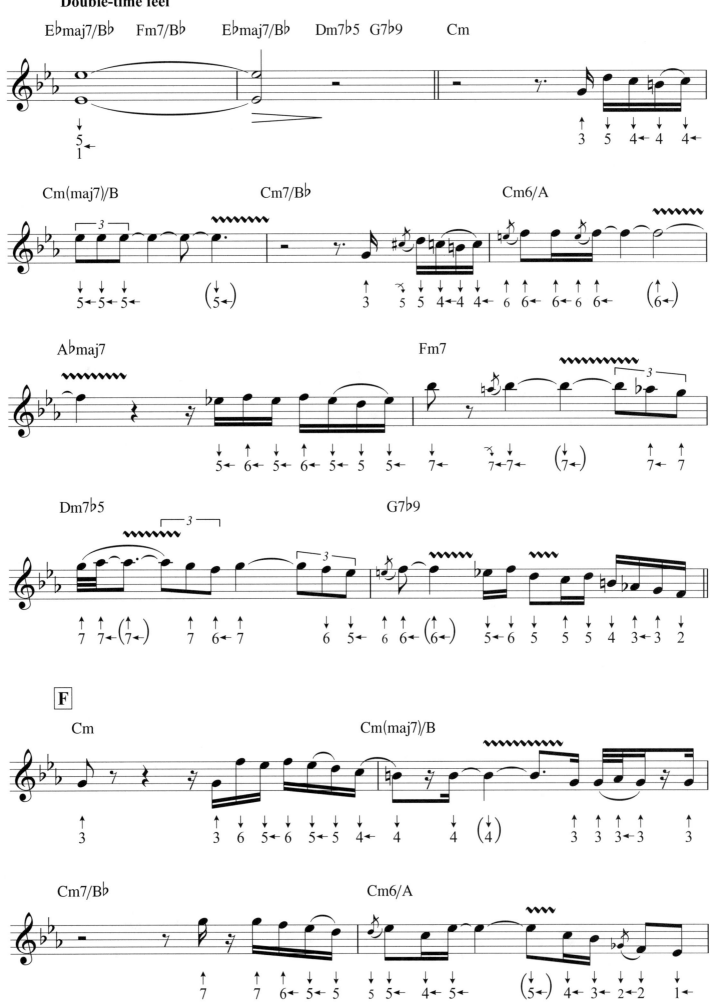

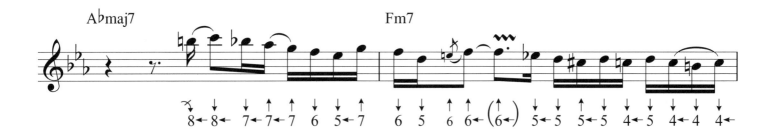

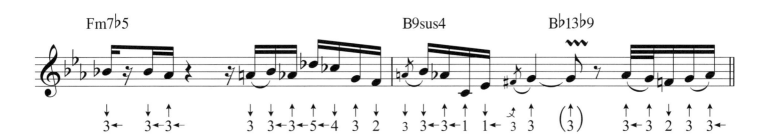

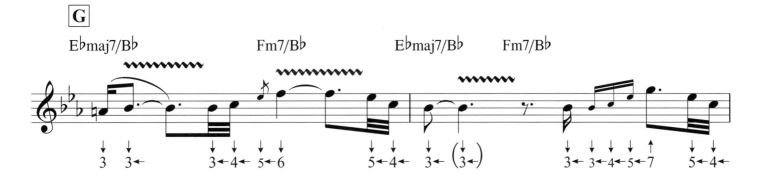

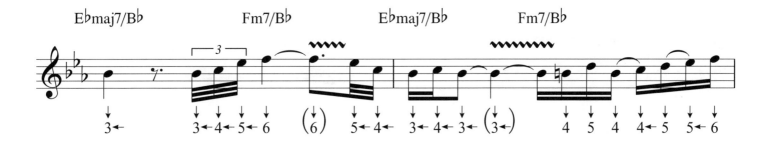

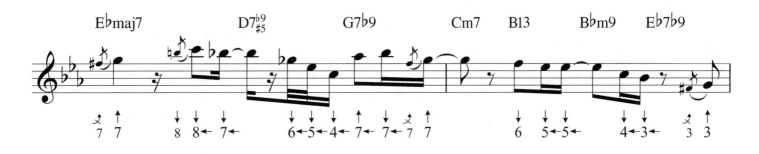

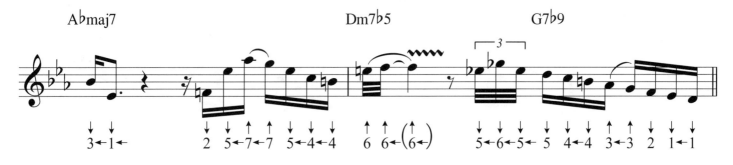

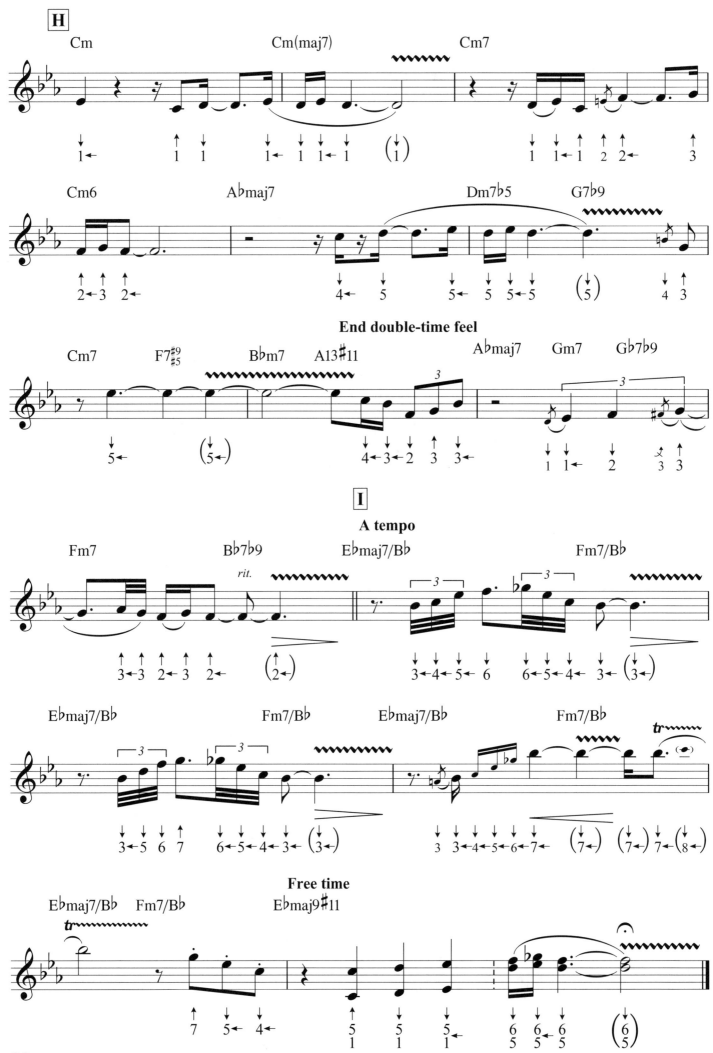

Satin Doll

By Duke Ellington

*Slide depressed half-way

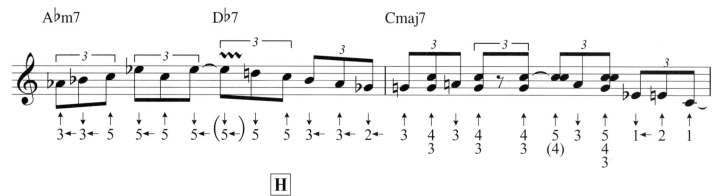

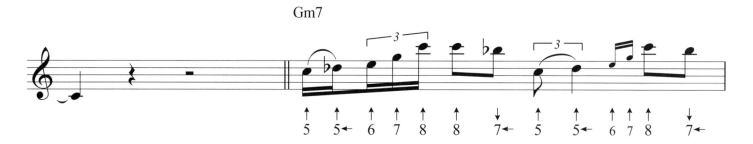

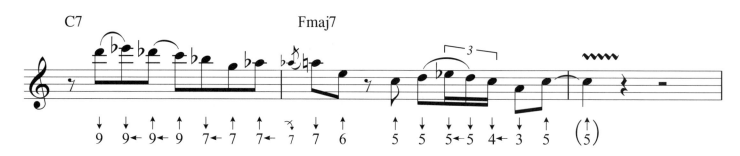

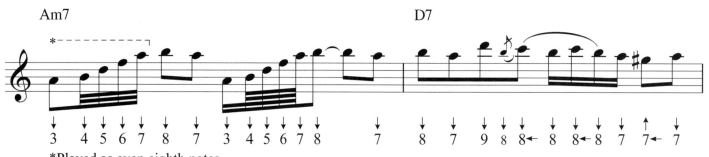

*Played as even eighth notes.

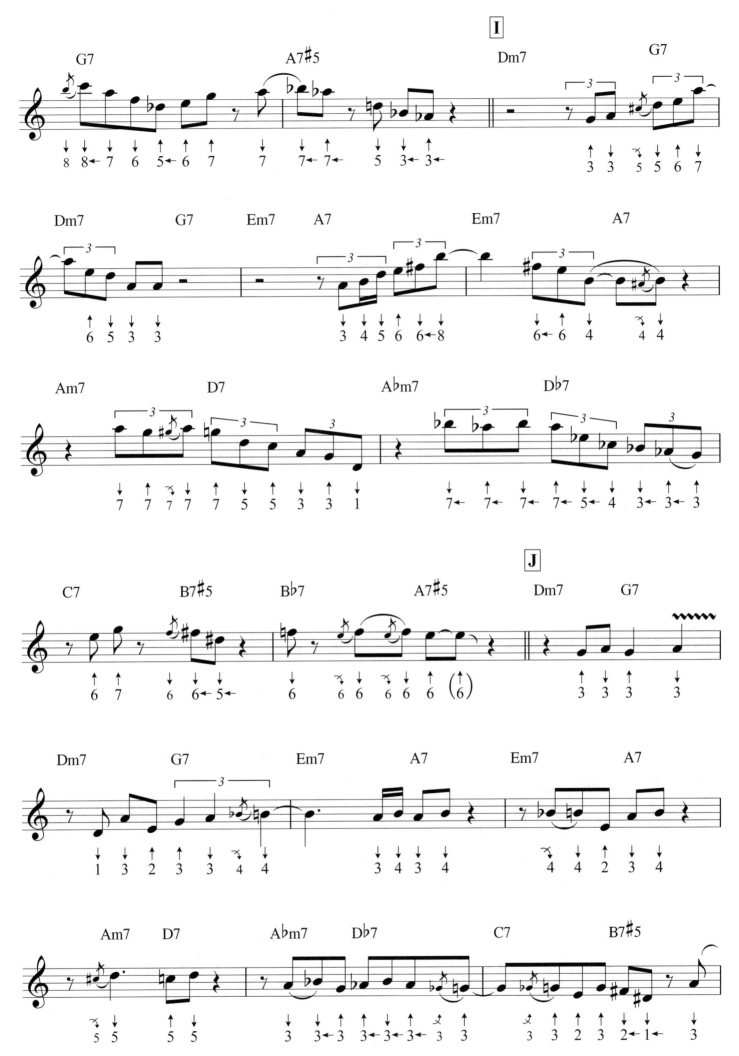

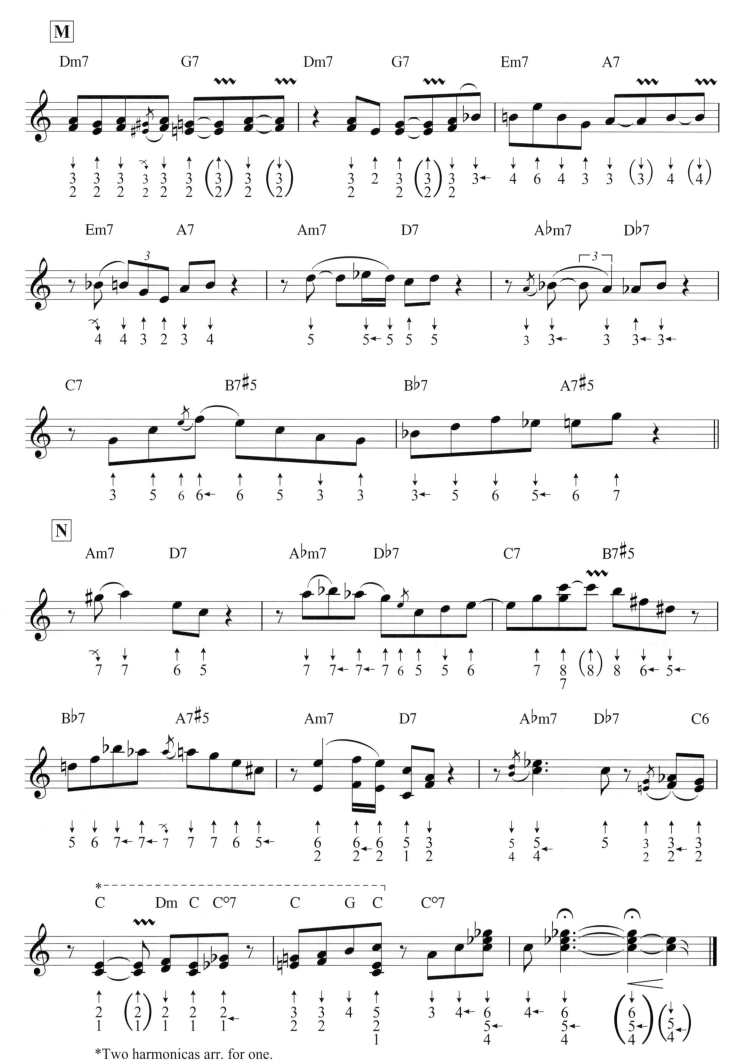

*Two harmonicas arr. for one.

Some Day My Prince Will Come

Words by Larry Morey
Music by Frank Churchill

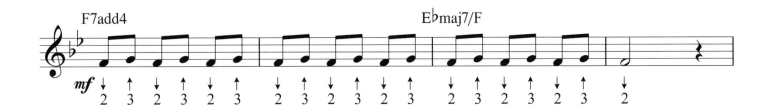

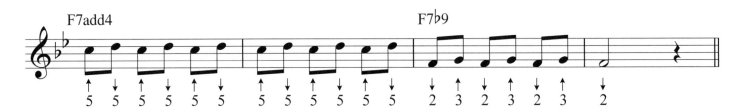

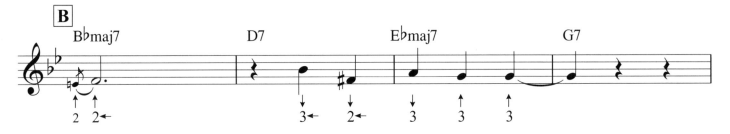

*Played behind the beat.

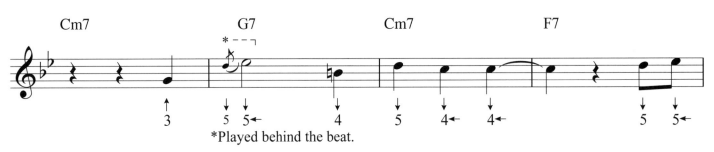

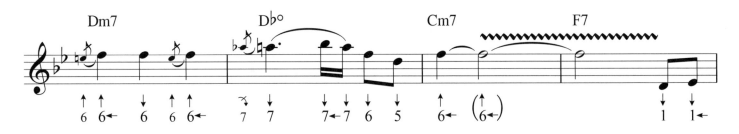

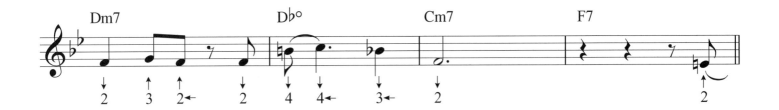

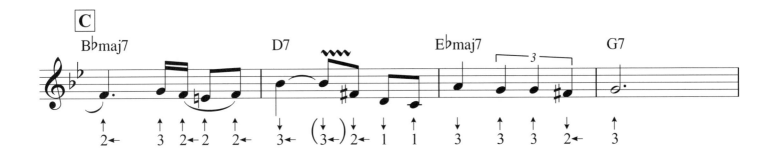

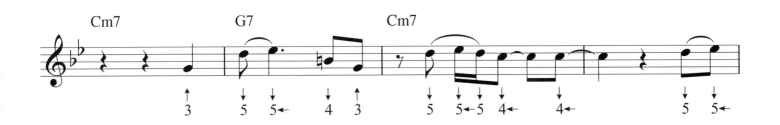

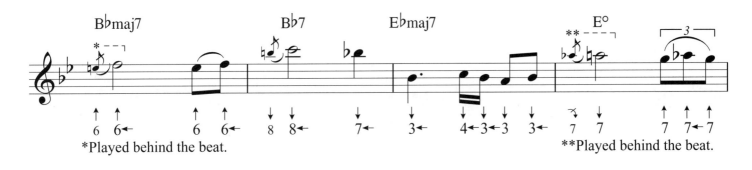

*Played behind the beat.   **Played behind the beat.

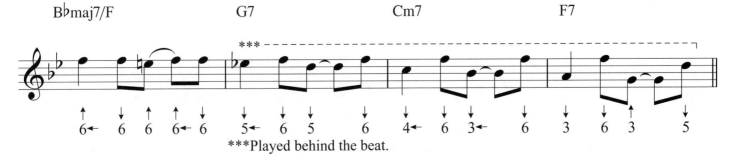

***Played behind the beat.

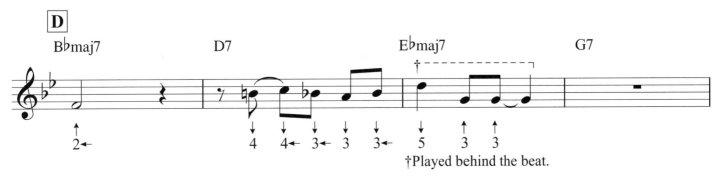

†Played behind the beat.

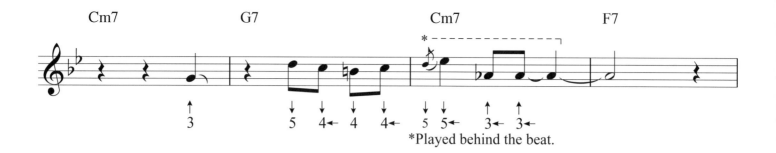

*Played behind the beat.

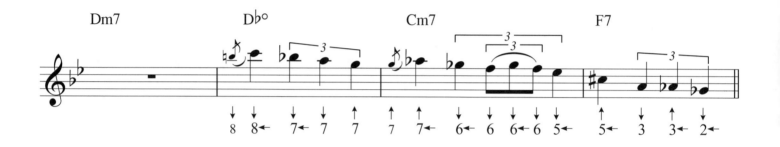

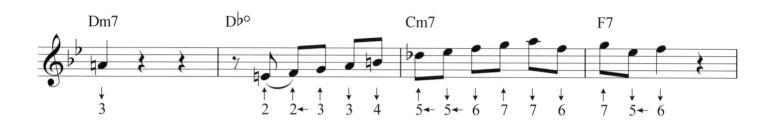

E

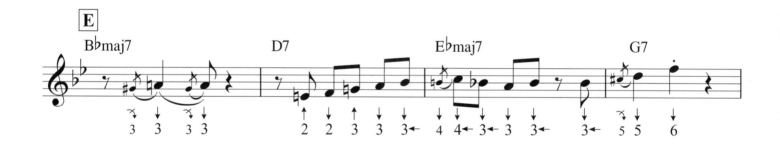

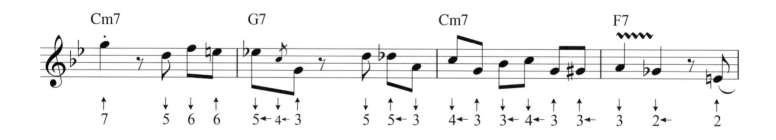

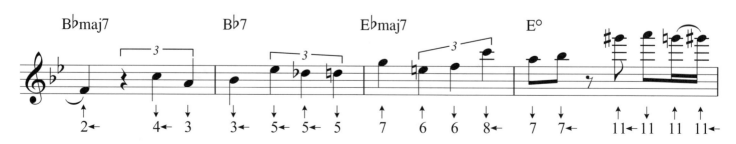

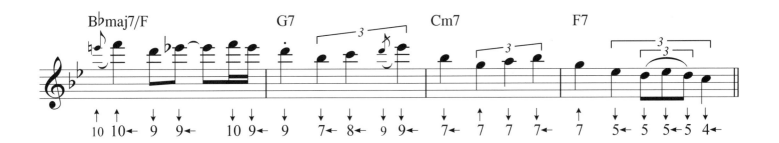

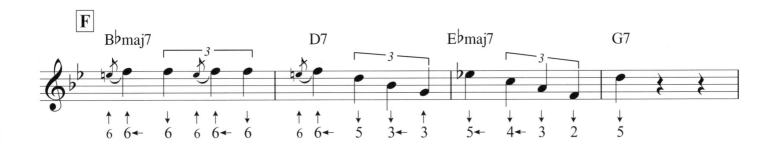

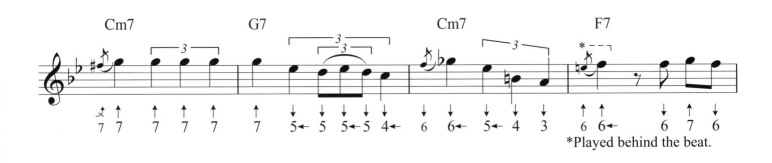

*Played behind the beat.

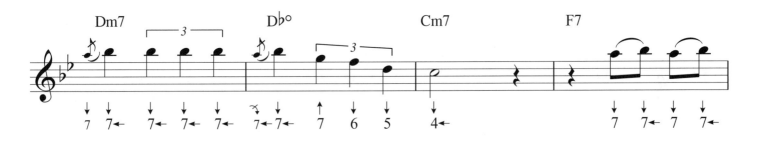

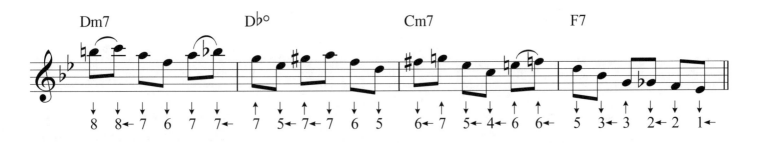

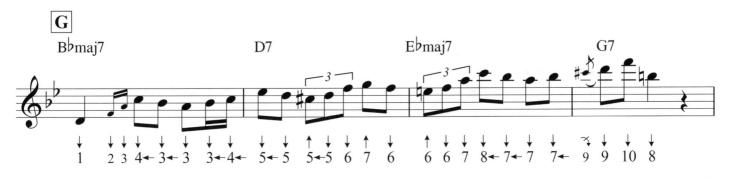

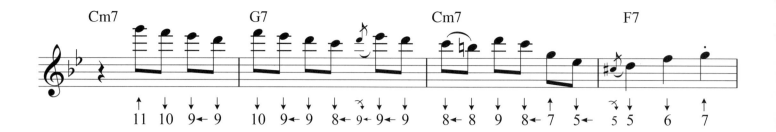

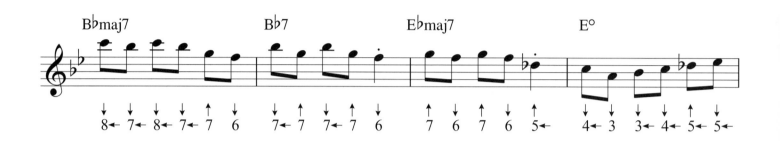

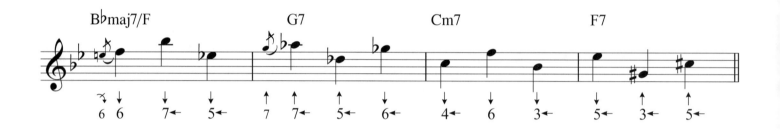

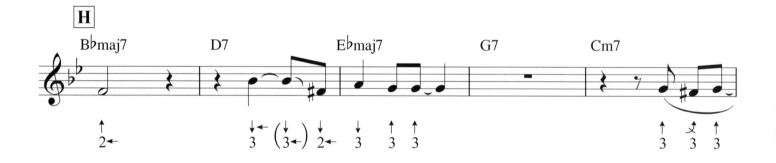

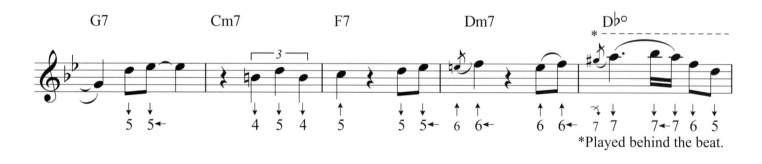

*Played behind the beat.

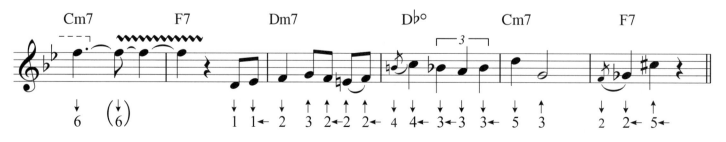

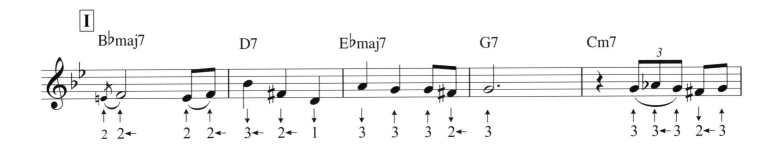

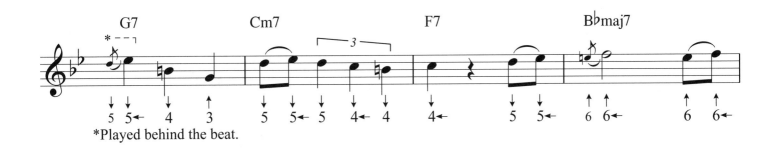

*Played behind the beat.

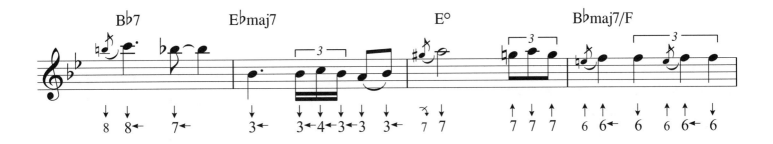

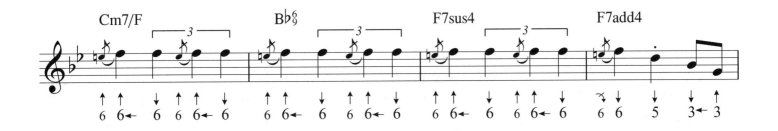

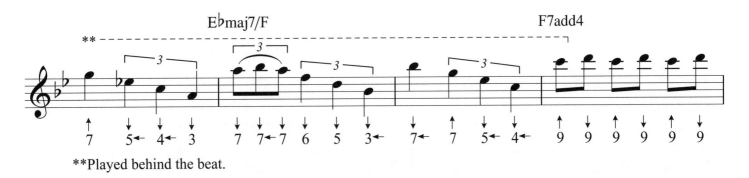

**Played behind the beat.

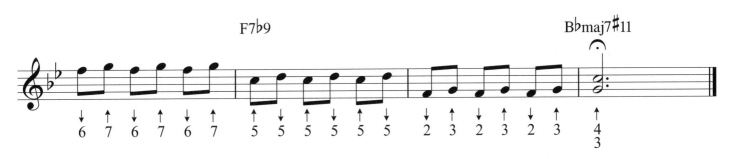

What a Wonderful World

Words and Music by George David Weiss and Bob Thiele

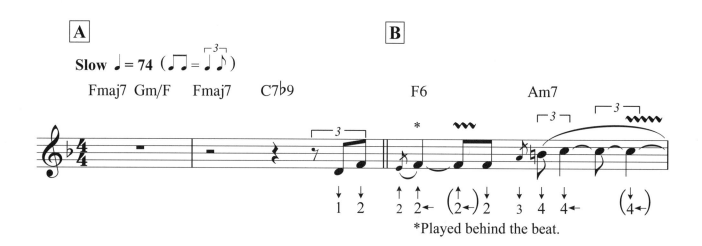

*Played behind the beat.

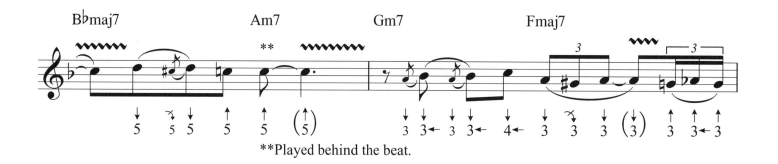

**Played behind the beat.

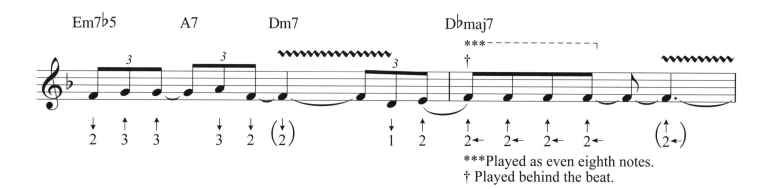

***Played as even eighth notes.
† Played behind the beat.

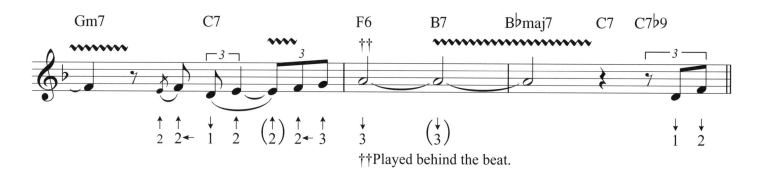

††Played behind the beat.

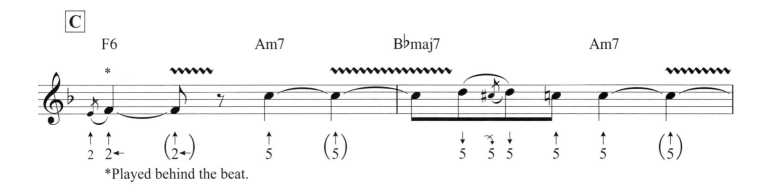

*Played behind the beat.

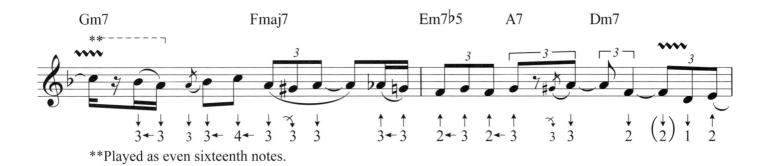

**Played as even sixteenth notes.

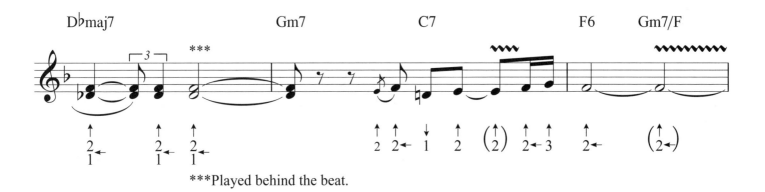

***Played behind the beat.

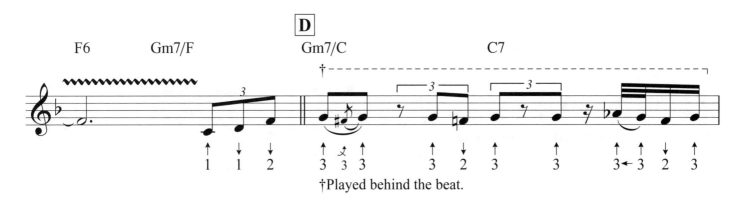

†Played behind the beat.

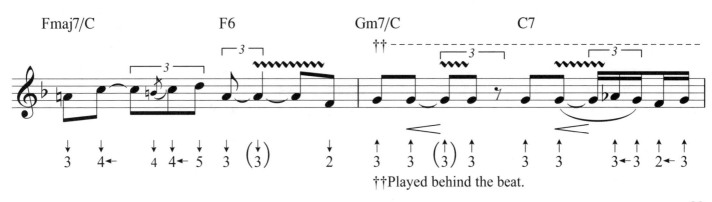

††Played behind the beat.

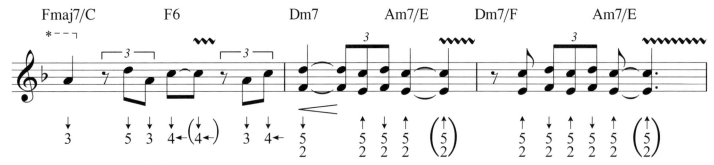

*Played behind the beat.

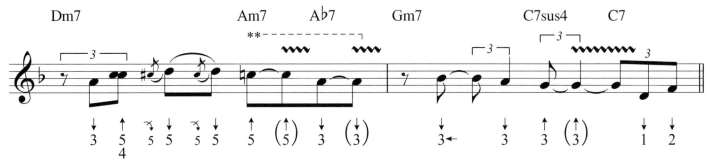

**Played behind the beat.

E

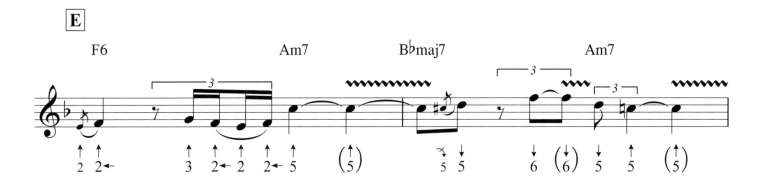

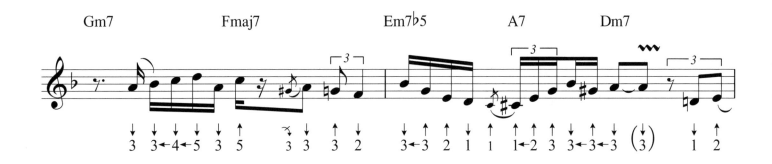

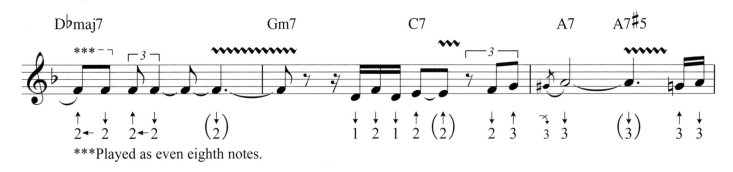

***Played as even eighth notes.

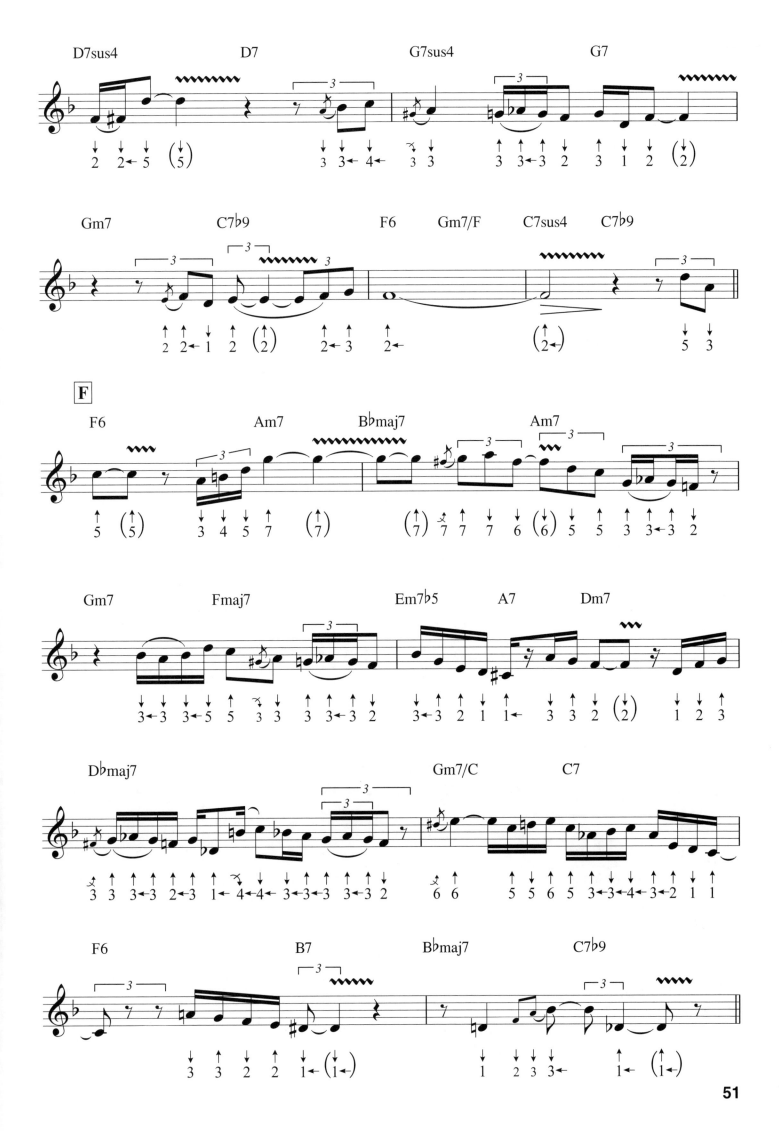

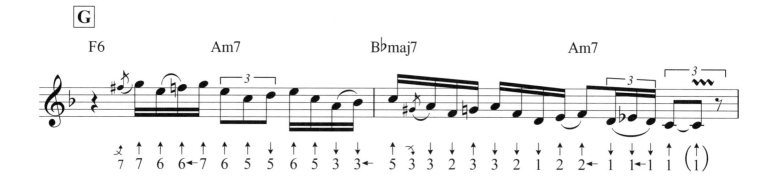

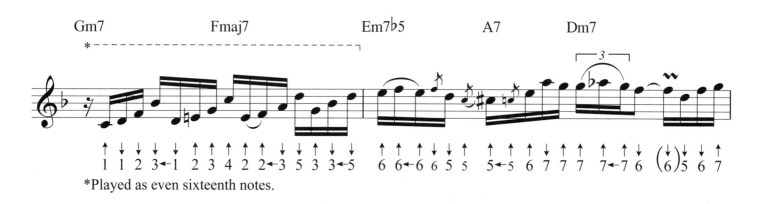

*Played as even sixteenth notes.

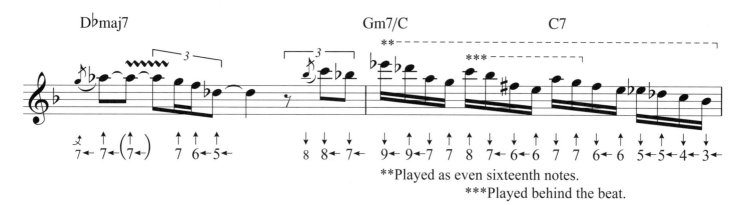

**Played as even sixteenth notes.
***Played behind the beat.

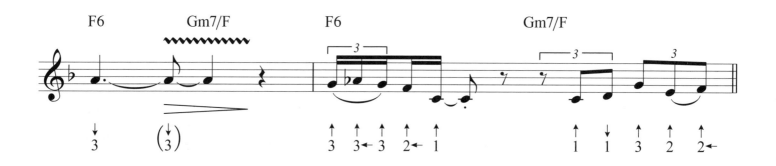

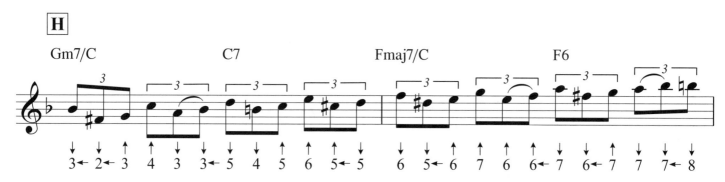

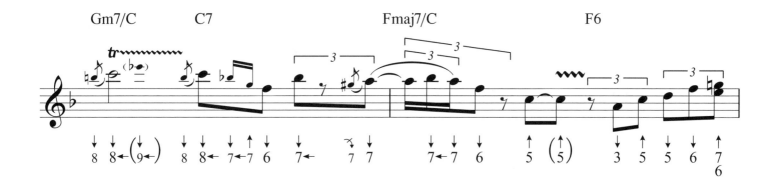

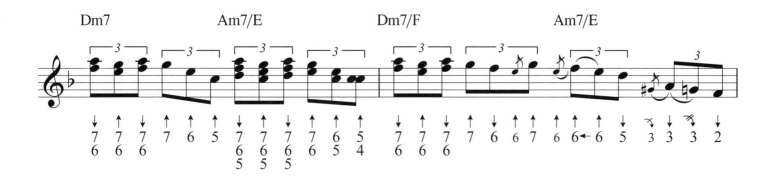

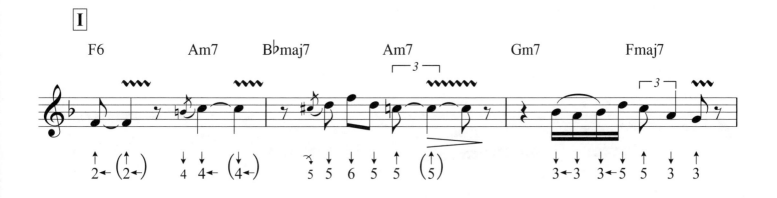

I

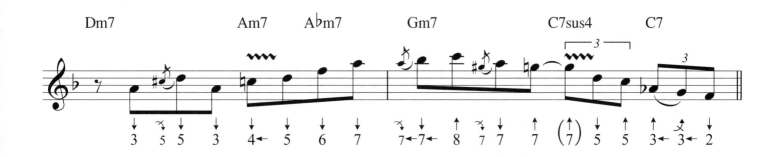

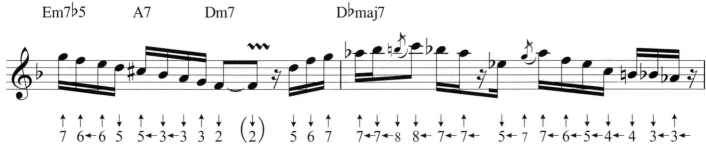

*Played behind the beat.

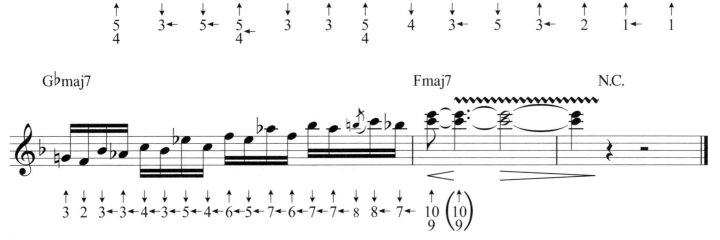

CHROMATIC HARMONICA NOTATION LEGEND

Harmonica music can be notated two different ways: on a *musical staff*, and in *tablature*.

THE MUSICAL STAFF shows pitches and rhythms and is divided by bar lines into measures. Pitches are named after the first seven letters of the alphabet.

TABLATURE graphically represents the harmonica music. Each note will be accompanied by a number, 1 through 12, indicating what hole you are to play. The arrow above indicates whether to blow or draw. (All examples are shown using a C chromatic harmonica.)

Notes:

Tab:

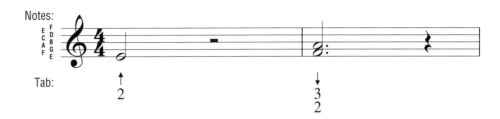

Blow (exhale) into 2nd hole.　　　Draw (inhale) 2nd & 3rd holes together.

Blow into 2nd hole while holding the slide in.　　　Draw 4th & 8th holes together while holding the slide in.

Notes on the 12-Hole C Chromatic Harmonica

Exhaled (Blown) Notes with Slide Out

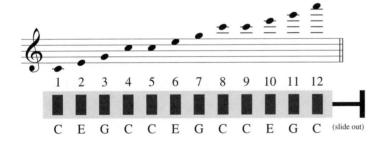

Inhaled (Drawn) Notes with Slide Out

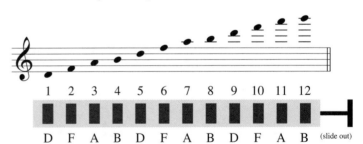

Exhaled (Blown) Notes with Slide In

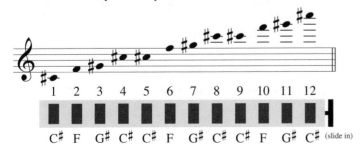

Inhaled (Drawn) Notes with Slide In

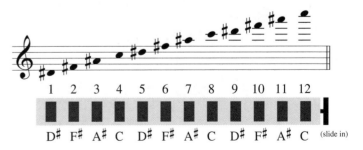

Definitions for Special Harmonica Notation

VIBRATO: Begin adding vibrato to the sustained note on beat 3.

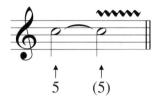

5   (5)

TONGUE BLOCKING: Using your tongue to block holes 2 & 3, play octaves on holes 1 & 4.

4
1

TRILL: Shake the harmonica rapidly to alternate between notes.

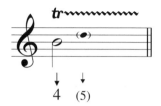

4   (5)

NOTE: Tablature numbers in parentheses are used when:

- The note is sustained, but a new articulation begins (such as vibrato), or
- The quantity of notes being sustained changes, or
- A change in dynamics (volume) occurs.
- It's the alternate note in a trill.

Additional Musical Definitions

D.S. al Coda
- Go back to the sign (𝄋), then play until the measure marked "***To Coda***," then skip to the section labelled "**Coda**."

 (accent)
- Accentuate the note (play initial attack louder).

D.C. al Fine
- Go back to the beginning of the song and play until the measure marked "***Fine***" (end).

 (staccato)
- Play the note short.

- Repeat measures between signs.

- When a repeated section has different endings, play the first ending only the first time and the second ending only the second time.

Dynamics

p
- Piano (soft)

mp
- Mezzo Piano (medium soft)

mf
- Mezzo Forte (medium loud)

f
- Forte (loud)

(crescendo)
- Gradually louder

(decrescendo)
- Gradually softer